IMAGES
*of America*

# CURTISS-WRIGHT

Between 1939 and 1945, the public was thirsty for information about Curtiss-Wright's newsmaking war-winners. Carefully skirting security concerns, "Curt Wright" did his best to slake their thirst.

IMAGES
*of America*

# CURTISS-WRIGHT

Kirk W. House

Published by Arcadia Publishing
Charleston SC, Chicago IL, Portsmouth NH, San Francisco CA

Printed in Great Britain

Library of Congress Catalog Card Number: 2005933531

For all general information contact Arcadia Publishing at:
Telephone 843-853-2070
Fax 843-853-0044
E-mail sales@arcadiapublishing.com
For customer service and orders:
Toll-Free 1-888-313-2665

Visit us on the Internet at http://www.arcadiapublishing.com

*Dedicated to the memory of my friend*
*Robert G. Bitgood*
*who at 16 was flying his Dad's Curtiss Robin*
*above the beaches of Rhode Island and at 20*
*was flying a Republic P-47 Thunderbolt*
*in dubious battle above the plains of Europe.*

*February 10, 1924–January 25, 2005*
*84 sorties in wartime*
*81 years of enthusiastic life*

# CONTENTS

# ACKNOWLEDGMENTS

For six years and five months, I had the great fun of being director and/or curator of the Glenn Curtiss Museum in Glenn's hometown of Hammondsport, New York. With a very few exceptions (noted in the captions), all the images in this book come from Curtiss Museum archives, to which I was graciously granted access by executive director Trafford L. M. Doherty and associate curator Rick Leisenring.

While these photographs and other materials came from many sources, I am honored to mention (as I have in several previous books) my gratitude for the collection donated by Lou Casey, an outstanding scholar of Curtiss and, indeed, of all aviation history. Those who want more detail on company history could not do better than *Curtiss-Wright: Greatness and Decline*, by Ed Young and Lou Eltscher. You can find encyclopedic airplane information in *Curtiss Aircraft: 1907–1947*, by Peter Bowers. Curtiss-Wright and its various divisions also put out internal magazines for many years, making a constantly unrolling panorama of company life and history.

Of course, Curtiss-Wright's life and history are far from over, and we are very grateful to Paul Ferdenzi (Associate General Counsel and Assistant Secretary), Jane Winter, Marek Syska, and Jason Otani for helping us out with images and information on Curtiss-Wright today. My son Joshua House, who has volunteered many hours in the museum archives, was, as he has often been before, a tremendous help with this book. Finally ten gold stars to editor Kaia Motter, for all her help and support. Without her, this book would have been far shorter!

*Nomenclature Note*
Curtiss-Wright repeatedly recycled product names—several Condors, Shrikes, and Hellcats are mentioned in the text. Various militaries often applied their own names (some official, some informal) to Curtiss aircraft, besides having official alphanumeric designations as well as the company's own internal model numbers. I have tried to use the most accessible designations whenever possible. Though the term P-40, for instance, technically refers to the company's Model 81 Hawk in U.S. Army service only, it is used here as the general term regardless of operator. I also most often use the overall designation without specifying the various sub- (and even subsub!) types.

# INTRODUCTION

Few 20th century tales are more exciting than the lives of Glenn Curtiss and the Wright brothers, including the bitter legal disputes that consumed them for a decade. But the story is bigger than even these three very big men.

Wilbur Wright died in 1912, and Orville Wright severed connections with Wright Aeronautical during the First World War. At just about the same time, Glenn Curtiss sold controlling interest in his own company. While Curtiss remained active as a board member and as head of several subsidiary corporations, his main interests now lay elsewhere.

But their companies—each of which began with an 1890s bike shop—continued to grow. A 1929 Wall Street merger created the gigantic Curtiss-Wright Corporation, with interests in engines, airframes, airports, airlines, flight schools, flying services, research, development . . . every aspect of aeronautics. The Depression shook the company to its foundations, but company leaders soldiered on, making Curtiss-Wright a major component of America's World War II "arsenal of democracy."

And still Curtiss-Wright thrives, more than 75 years since the great merger, more than a century since three forward-looking young men went into business—and into dreaming—for themselves. Where Curtiss and the Wrights were once delighted to get off the ground at all, Curtiss-Wright now sails into space, under the sea, into combat, and all around the globe. If Curtiss and the Wrights were here today, they would be jostling for window seats.

In war and in peace, anywhere men and women could fly, Curtiss-Wright took them there.

# One

# The Best Things with Wings

The oldest names in aviation came together in 1929 as the Curtiss Aeroplane and Motor Corporation merged with the Wright Aeronautical Corporation, both companies sweeping up numerous smaller firms in their wake. Curtiss-Wright was America's second-biggest company, surpassed only by General Motors. Glenn Curtiss had vaulted to the forefront of America's aviation business as early as 1909–1910, and though he was no longer at the company's helm, Curtiss airplanes were still industry leaders. Curtiss-Wright, along with the rest of the world, was embarking on a wild ride that would take it from open-cockpit biplanes to sleek, advanced war birds in scarcely a single decade. The Depression would quickly dim grand dreams of a gigantic, full-service business covering every aspect of aviation. But for far too short a time, the Curtiss Condor II airliner, soaring above the Empire State Building, perfectly captured the Golden Age of flight.

Clement Keys of Curtiss along with Richard Hoyt at Wright Aeronautical engineered the merger. Keys headed up the new corporation.

Hoyt and Keys had already begun recreating their respective firms as conglomerates, so the merger was a logical next step. The symbolism on this celebratory plaque would probably be found odd today.

The first official Curtiss-Wright (C-W) aircraft was the CW-1 Junior, a 570-pound airplane with a three-cylinder engine and a pusher propeller. Walter Beech headed up the project, with orders to bring it in at no more than $1,500 retail. The sticker price was $1,495.

Juniors sold well at first, even in the Depression, but several widely publicized accidents (resulting from mishandling, rather than from inherent flaws) soured the market. Despite the Junior's popularity, dreams of finding one in every driveway next to the Model T withered away. Shown here, pilot Jack Jeffords (left) and shotgunner Claud Kimball hunt coyotes from their Junior near Broken Bow, Nebraska.

Glenn Curtiss invented the first practical seaplane back in 1911, so a Junior on floats was no surprise 20 years later. But it must have been hard to get aloft with that tiny engine.

J. Maitland Bleecker's experimental helicopter was a carry-over project from before the merger. C-W dropped the program when the prototype wrecked on a test flight. Bleecker was still living in the late 1990s.

The tiny Model 58 (Navy F9C) Sparrowhawk fighter had an unusual hook arrangement above the cockpit.

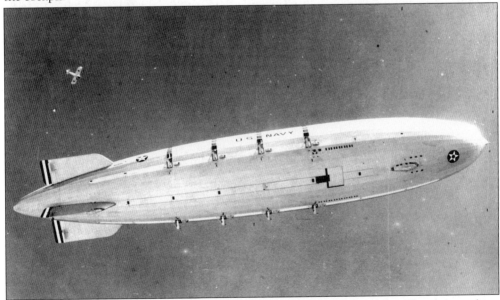

Fast airplanes had short ranges, while slow dirigibles could circle the globe. The obvious thing to do was to drop Sparrowhawks from the opening in the airship's keel. When "the Men on the Flying Trapeze" returned from their missions, the airship lowered a bar. The Sparrowhawk pilots flew underneath, hooked on in flight, and were cranked inside. Landing gear was optional.

Advancing technology ensured that the system was never tested in war (thank goodness). There's a persistent legend that Sparrowhawks toppled King Kong; sad to relate, it isn't true.

Curtiss test pilots, identified from left to right as Croswell, Johnson, Boyd, and Ogden, took a break from their dangerous labors on September 3, 1931.

Enthusiastic though the company was over civil designs, the Depression ensured that much of the business would be military, including the Model 52 (Army B-2) Condor, which at one point constituted the entire heavy bomber force. Several Condors are leading this 1930 flight at Presidio's Crissy Field.

C-W pinned high hopes on the passenger version of the Condor.

Many engineers already considered the original Condor a little old-fashioned, but it was certainly a dramatic advance on the first Wright Flyer, just 25 years earlier. Pilots pivoted the wheel from one to the other.

C-W board member Glenn Curtiss piloted a Condor from Albany to Buffalo in 1930, reprising his famous flight that he had made 20 years earlier in a fragile open pusher. Two months later, the company's namesake unexpectedly died at the age of 52.

The contemporary Patrician airliner from Keystone (a subsidiary brought in as part of Wright Aeronautical's dowry) was far more advanced. The trimotor configuration, as opposed to the Condor's twin-engine setup, enhanced confidence but demolished comfort, since the nose engine transmitted noise and vibration all through the cabin.

Another Wright subsidiary made the Gypsy Moth, which was far more famous in its military trainer version.

*Tradewind*, a Wright Aeronautical magazine, assured readers that "The Gypsy Moth, with folded wings, fits into the average single-car garage nicely." If nothing else, this demonstrates how common home garages had become by 1930.

Curtiss-Reid manufactured the Reid Rambler in Canada between 1928 and 1931.

Work in such remote operations as mines took on new dimensions with the introduction of air service.

Admiral Byrd liked the sleek, updated Condor II, using it for Atlantic flights and Antarctic expeditions. Notice that the Curtiss airframe has a Wright power plant. Too bad they hadn't gotten around to buying Edo!

Polar flying placed extreme demands on ships and men alike.

Aircraft would be fitted with floats, wheels, or skis as occasion required. This Condor was abandoned in the Antarctic in 1941. Similar civil versions with retractable wheels were used as sleeper airliners.

Marine Capt. Arthur H. Page thrilled crowds by winning the last Curtiss Marine Trophy (for seaplanes) in a Curtiss F6C-3. The award, donated personally by Glenn Curtiss, was discontinued after his death two months later. Page was later killed racing a Curtiss Hawk fighter plane.

The navy's pre-merger F7C-1 Seahawk also set imaginations aflame.

Curtiss Army Hawks raced at Crissy Field in the Presidio in 1930. Besides stimulating taxpayer enthusiasm, air racing tested the limits of pilots and machines.

Army Lt. Jimmy Doolittle, shown here in Shanghai, enthusiastically demonstrated his Curtiss Hawk fighter (or pursuit plane, in contemporary parlance) across the globe. Besides running world-record races in Curtiss machines, Doolittle flew C-W sales exhibitions in South America and China.

Just as the Curtiss-Wright merger was taking place, Capt. Ross G. Hoyt flew the Hawk XP-6B "Hoyt Special" from Mitchell Field, Long Island to Nome, Alaska, in 34 hours and 20 minutes. The Hoyt Special had a liquid-cooled Curtiss Conqueror engine.

The two-seater Curtiss Falcon had numerous applications, including the army A-3 ground attack configuration.

Capt. William Kepner, who tested a new machine-gun mount on his Falcon, later made lieutenant general, leading the Eighth Fighter Command in World War II.

This single-seat Falcon with air-cooled Wright Cyclone engine flew airmail in South America.

That plane was previously owned by Charles A. Lindbergh, who used it in a liquid-cooled, two-seat version to make surveys for Curtiss subsidiary Transcontinental Air Transport.

This liquid-cooled float plane version, from just before the merger, demonstrates the versatility of this type of aircraft. Between them, Peru and Columbia fielded over 100 Falcons for their war in 1932–1934.

The navy F8C Hell-Diver dive-bomber was another carryover from pre-merger days. Assistant Navy Secretary David Ingalls used this unit with its Wright Cyclone engine as a personal transport.

During the Depression, consolidation forced the closure of the Curtiss Engineering Corporation, including this model shop.

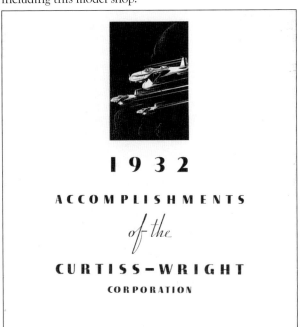

**1932**

**ACCOMPLISHMENTS**

*of the*

**CURTISS—WRIGHT**

**CORPORATION**

With civil sales faltering during the Depression, the 1932 annual report emphasized the Shrike army dive-bomber.

Some of the modelers moved from Long Island to the main plant in Buffalo. The Shrike is shown on the table.

As an industry leader, Curtiss-Wright maintained extensive training establishments.

Though more or less stagnant, like most industries during the 1930s, as Europe rearmed, aviation looked more and more like a growth field.

Robert R. Osborn (left) was project engineer on the Tanager, which won $100,000 in the Guggenheim Safe Plane Competition. Theodore P. "Ted" Wright (right), no relation to the famous brothers who no longer had any involvement with the company, was a leading engineer, first for Curtiss and then for C-W.

Despite such dramatic innovations as wing-length flaps, the Tanager's advanced features were too costly for general use in the Depression.

Engineers performed critical calculations without even a dream of computers.

Curtiss-Wright got some reflected glory in 1938 when Douglas Corrigan "accidentally" flew his pre-merger Curtiss Robin from Long Island, not to his announced destination of California, but to Ireland—a flight plan that safety-conscious aviation officials had repeatedly vetoed. Schoolboys who recognized him outside the Board of Trade in London bagged autographs. "Wrong-Way" Corrigan still owned his Robin (*Sunshine*) at his death in 1995.

The Model 77 navy SBC Hell-Diver, while far advanced from its predecessor of the same name, was still in production in 1940, by which time it was just about obsolete. The SBC4 subtype (like this one) had an 850-horsepower Wright engine. This was the navy's last combat biplane, and Marines were using them as late as 1943. The British called them Clevelands.

VOL. XXII No. 2
SUMMER 1938

A PUBLICATION OF CURTISS AEROPLANE DIVISION ... CURTISS-WRIGHT CORPORATION BUFFALO, NEW YORK

# *Curtiss* FLY LEAF

The SOC Seagull operated from navy cruisers and battleships, deployed by catapult for scouting and observation.

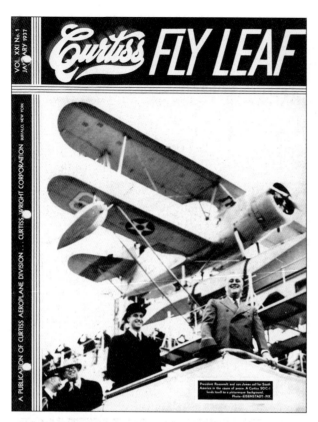

VOL. XXI No. 1 JANUARY 1937

Curtiss FLY LEAF

A PUBLICATION OF CURTISS AEROPLANE DIVISION . . . CURTISS-WRIGHT CORPORATION  BUFFALO, NEW YORK

President Roosevelt and son James sail for South America in the cause of peace. A Curtiss SOC-1 lends itself to a picturesque background.
Photo-EISENSTADT-PIX

This Seagull may have reminded Pres. Franklin D. Roosevelt of his first airplane ride, which he took when he was the assistant navy secretary. He made the trip in a Curtiss flying boat during World War I. James Roosevelt is standing to his father's right.

The 1935 CW-19 was an advanced, all-metal private plane that found few takers. Two dozen of the military fighter version with Wright Whirlwind engines were sold to China and Latin America.

The small CW-21 Demon light fighter had a huge Wright Cyclone engine, demanding a rather odd fuselage configuration. Dutch Demons fought the Japanese in the East Indies.

Three-dozen CW-22 Falcons wound up in Australia after the East Indies fell. Turkey bought 50, while the U.S. Navy took 150 as trainers. The light fighter concept, while seductive, was ultimately unfruitful. Since they took just as much time to engineer and produce as heavier models, they were only marginally less expensive while far less powerful. The Falcon, for instance, carried just two guns.

By 1939, galloping technology and impending war were devouring more and more of the company's resources. Even so, in 1940, the 36-passenger CW-20 sub-stratospheric, pressurized airliner seemed to poise Curtiss-Wright for a promising future in civil aviation. History had other plans.

# Two

# ANYWHERE, ANYTIME

Designing, engineering, and manufacturing were the heart of Curtiss-Wright, but sales were its lifeblood. It was understandable for the oldest names in aviation to also handle airlines, airports, flying schools, and flying services. The new Curtiss-Wright was never a monopoly—there were too many other players in the game—but it did establish a glorious vertical consolidation that might have rationalized the business if the Depression had not shattered C-W's dreams along with so many others. But, for a breathtaking moment, Americans could go "anywhere, anytime" with Curtiss-Wright.

*Curtiss-Wright Instructor Discussing Aerial Maneuvers With A Group of Flying Students*

# CURTISS-WRIGHT FLYING COURSES

CURTISS-WRIGHT standardized courses of flight instruction are the result of the experience gained by the outstanding military and commercial pilots of America. They are designed in conformity with the highest requirements of the United States Department of Commerce.

Glenn Curtiss and the Wright brothers started commercial flying schools in 1910. By the 1930s, it had already become crystal clear that instruction, and hangar talk, called for masterly hand motions.

The Flying Service (instruction, service, and charters) used, among other aircraft, the Sikorsky S-38 amphibian. Sikorsky was a C-W subsidiary.

The C-W school in Chicago offered instruction on the Mercury Chic, with an option to buy. The Chic was designed and manufactured by old Curtiss hands in Glenn Curtiss's hometown of Hammondsport, New York. The program and the aircraft were well thought of, but business was sluggish during the Depression.

| | | | | | |
|---|---|---|---|---|---|
| Aeroplanes Available at All Times | | | **NO.** | | |
| Commercial Flying, Land or Water | | **CURTISS-WRIGHT FLYING SERVICE, INC.** | | | |
| Freight and Passengers | | Valley Stream N.Y. **AIRPORT** | | | |
| Aerial Photography | | | | | |
| Cross Country | **TO** Mr. Paul H. Quick | | **DATE** November 14th 1930. | | |
| Schools | | | | | |

| | | | | | |
|---|---|---|---|---|---|
| **TERMS NET** | | **VIA** | **YOUR ORDER NO.** | | |
| **QUANTITY** | **NO.** | **DESCRIPTION** | **UNIT PRICE** | **NET AMOUNT** | |
| | | 11-13-30 W.O. B-372-- Replace exhaust valve Gudies and seats. | | | |
| | | in Ox-5 Cylinders. Reface Valves. | | | |
| | 16 | valve Guides | 42 00 | | |
| | 8 | valve seats. | 33 60 | | |
| | 1½ | hrs. Mechanics 'Time @$2.00-hr. | 3 00 | | |
| | | | $ | 78 60 | |

The Flying Service also handled repairs . . . for instance, on elderly Curtiss OX-5 engines. Most aviation mechanics get more than two dollars an hour nowadays.

The Flying Service highlighted three of its offerings at the February 1930 International Aircraft Exposition in St. Louis. From left to right are the Curtiss Kingbird, Keystone-Loening Commuter flying boat (resting in a pool of water), and Curtiss Tanager. Their setting seems aimed at tempting customers to fly to sunnier climates.

CURTIS-WRIGHT AIRPORT NEAR SINGAC, N. J.

Curtiss-Wright also operated airports around the country.

Seaplane runs to Cuba and the Bahamas were always popular. Until Prohibition was repealed, it is just possible that some return trips carried liquor on board.

Curtiss workers had their own glider club, at least for a while.

The summer camp on Martha's Vineyard was aptly named as students slept under canvas. Learners typically flew the front cockpit in these tandem two-seaters, right about at the center of gravity. When alone, the pilot maintained balance by flying from the rear.

CURTISS
WRIGHT
FLYING
COURSES

GROUND SCHOOL
AND AVIATION
MECHANICS' COURSES

FLY

OVER
NEW YORK

DAILY
SIGHTSEEING
SERVICE

CURTISS-WRIGHT FLYING SERVICE
CALDWELL · VALLEY STREAM · FLUSHING

The open sky and the open cockpit kindled the same dreams that the lonesome locomotive whistle had sparked a generation earlier. As the railroad had been, the airplane and the Brooklyn Bridge were perfectly matched as exemplars of exciting, well-loved, forward-leaping technology.

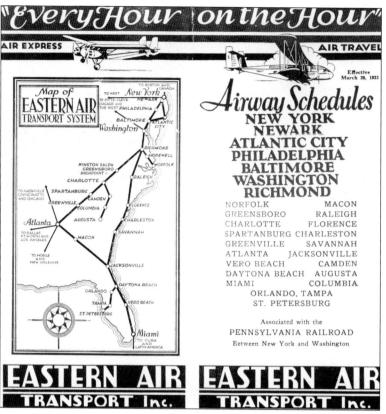

C-W was heavily invested in Eastern Air Transport (EAT).

Eastern's Curtiss Condor II Airliners would carry passengers from Newark to Miami for $73.67. Bus fare from the Governor Clinton Hotel in New York City was 75¢. The flight to Miami took 14 hours and 30 minutes, assuming all went well, of course.

EAT seemingly wanted to give an impression of solidity and permanence—qualities spectacularly lacking in many 1930s airlines.

Curtiss-Wright's National Air Transport flew airplanes that were surprisingly small by today's standards.

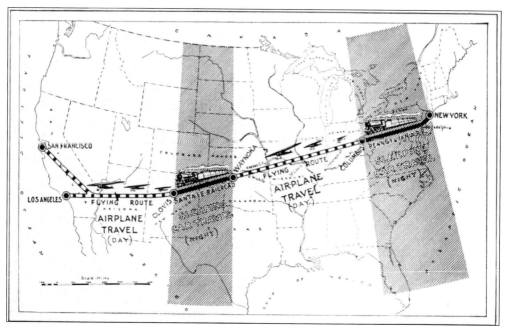

Transcontinental Air Transport, another associated company, faced the fact that most passengers feared flying by night. Alternating daylight flying with nighttime rail sleepers let passengers race from coast to coast in two days.

AIRPORT
LIGHTING
EQUIPMENT

Curtiss-Wright Airports Corporation    Airport Equipment Sales Department

Curtiss Airports took the lead in lighting their fields.

CURTISS·WRIGHT·
REYNOLDS AIRPORT

LOOP

## HOW TO REACH CURTISS-WRIGHT-REYNOLDS AIRPORT

If you plan to drive to the Races study the map and become familiar with the most convenient route to the Airport. Choose one around and not through the congested part of the city.

North Shore Line service direct to grandstand, 75c round trip. Trains will leave Adams and Wabash station at frequent intervals, stopping at all North Shore stations including Belmont Avenue, Wilson Avenue and Howard Street.

Chicago Milwaukee and St. Paul train service direct to the airport, 60c round trip. Trains will leave Union Station at frequent intervals between 12 M. and 1:20 P. M. Chicago daylight saving time.

It is recommended that you purchase your tickets in advance so as not to hold up traffic and to avoid unnecessary delay at the gates.

Consider that getting to the airport and returning is part of the enjoyment of the races. Make your plans accordingly.

### FREE AUTO PARKING

INTERNATIONAL
AIR RACES
AND
GORDON BENNETT BALLOON RACE

SEPT. 1·2·3·4
CHICAGO
CURTISS-REYNOLDS AIRPORT

SANCTIONED BY THE
NATIONAL AERONAUTIC ASS'N

SPONSORED BY
THE CHICAGO DAILY NEWS

THE OFFICIAL
COMPETITIVE AERONAUTICAL EVENT
A CENTURY OF PROGRESS

Curtiss promoted development of commercial and private fields, which would, of course, stimulate demand for all of their business segments. Standing room for the 1933 races at Curtiss-Reynolds Airport cost 50¢, including parking.

A 1930 air show at Curtiss-Reynolds had featured navy and army war birds from Curtiss.

Exhibitions and air meets had been vital sales venues as far back as the early days of the original Wright and Curtiss companies. Jimmy Doolittle was obviously delighted with his Curtiss Hawk.

Bargain Day at Grand Central Air Terminal, Los Angeles, Cal. "Penny-a-Pound" Rides attracted 20,000 people to the airport

Using 12 Ford Trimotors in Los Angeles, the Flying Service's "Penny-A-Pound—You Pay What You Weigh" promotion attracted 1,462 short-hop passengers over two days in 1930. Another 200 people took longer flights in smaller airplanes.

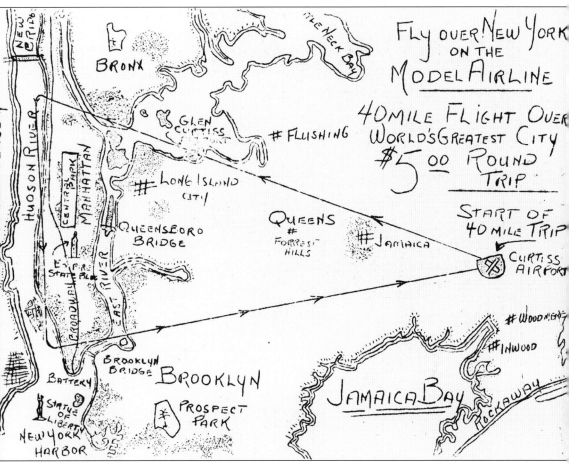

Glenn Curtiss Airport, now LaGuardia, was 15 minutes from downtown Manhattan by motorboat, which delivered passengers as close as possible to the Grand Central area. The "new bridge" was finally named after George Washington. "Fly Today," the reverse of this brochure urged, promising speeds of 110 miles an hour and "exhibition flying every Sunday." You would expect no less from the "world's oldest flying organization."

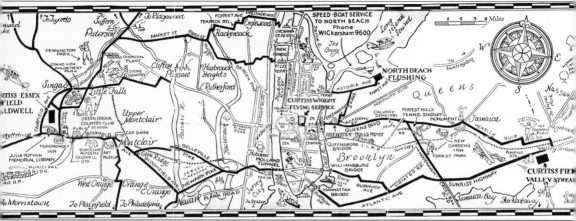

When New York City was America's capital of excitement and elegance, Curtiss-Wright Flying Service was its magic carpet. The North Beach seaplane base (later named for Glenn Curtiss) became LaGuardia Airport. Not long before this map was printed, Elinor Smith took off from Curtiss Field and flew under all four bridges on the East River, much to the official annoyance (and private delight) of Mayor "Gentleman Jimmy" Walker. Smith was 15 years old.

# *Three*

# CYCLONES, WHIRLWINDS, AND CONQUERORS

With business staggering after World War I, Wright Aeronautical shrewdly bought rights to the Lawrance radial engine, simultaneously securing the services of Charles Lawrance himself as a vice president. Both decisions were brilliant. Wright Aeronautical would elaborate the basic Lawrance design for a quarter century, creating air-cooled radial Whirlwinds, Cyclones, and other outstanding engines. Engine work at Curtiss lagged after the war, curiously so considering Glenn Curtiss's fame as an engine man as far back as 1903. By the time of the merger, Curtiss's only truly competitive engine was the liquid-cooled Conqueror, production of which was shifted over to Wright. As the Depression took its toll, Wright Aeronautical's engines became C-W's main moneymaker. But as war drew near, the obscure propeller division took on new life, and new significance, of its own.

Guy Warner Vaughn, an automotive engineer who entered aeronautics through Wright-Martin in World War I, became president of Wright Aeronautical in 1930. In World War II, he was president of Curtiss-Wright.

Folks at Curtiss were still fiddling with their considerable stock of 90-horsepower OX-5 engines left over from World War I. C. Roy Keys had this one installed in his car. Even competitive manufacturers often designed their airplanes around the ubiquitous OX-5.

The 12-cylinder Curtiss Conqueror was a fine, liquid-cooled engine in a day when air-cooling was placed at a premium.

Twelve Conquerors (six pushing, six pulling) powered the 150-passenger Dornier DO-X trans-Atlantic flying boat.

The six-cylinder Crusader, while respected, found few customers.

The pre-merger Curtiss Flying Service used an aircraft from an independent competitor (Fairchild) carrying a Curtiss Challenger engine, one of Curtiss's rare radial ventures before the merger.

The Wright radials, on the other hand, were industry leaders. In various sizes, they powered everything from small private aircraft to huge bombers, transports, and cargo planes.

**WRIGHT CYCLONE ENGINES**

**. . 575 H.P. . .**

**WRIGHT AERONAUTICAL CORPORATION**
PATERSON, NEW JERSEY • A Division of Curtiss-Wright

Lawrance's brainchild started out small but powerful. The horizontally opposed 90-horsepower twin cylinder Lawrance A-3 appeared in 1916. (Author's collection.)

By 1923, the Lawrance-Wright J-4B generated 200 horsepower. (Author's collection)

A Wright Whirlwind J-5C powered Charles A. Lindbergh and his *Spirit of St. Louis* on their way to Paris. Clarence Chamblerlin and Robert Byrd each flew from New York to Europe a month after Lindbergh. All three aircraft used J-5C Whirlwinds.

George Haldeman (third from left) took off minutes after this photograph was taken and set a world altitude record in a Bellanca Pacemaker with a Wright Whirlwind 300-horsepower engine. Elinor Smith (second from left) set her own world record two weeks later, using the same engine and a similar aircraft. Smith blacked out when her oxygen equipment failed, tumbling almost 20,000 feet before reviving and recovering safely. Flanking the pilots are Shirley Short (left) and R. B. C. Noorduyn.

A 235-horsepower Wright J-6-8 carried Wrong-Way Corrigan to Ireland in his rebuilt Curtiss Robin, Sunshine. The unit pictured still powers John Barker's 1930 Speedwing D-4000 from Travel Air, another C-W subsidiary. (Author's collection.)

The powerful radials grew to almost frightening size by 1937. The new Wright Cyclone R-2600, with its staggered cylinders, put out over 1,500 horsepower. Cyclones (over four feet in diameter) powered such big birds as the Boeing Pan Am Clipper, the Grumman TBF Avenger, the Curtiss SB2C Helldiver, the B-25 and A-20 bombers, and the Martin Mariner PBM flying boat. (Author's collection.)

As demand increased, the propeller division moved from Buffalo to Clifton, New Jersey, in 1938.

The division had its own internal magazine.

Electric propellers, which varied their pitch to suit conditions and improve performance, were an important advance from the early days of aeronautics. British and United States airmen alike learned the ropes from such instructors as Francis Richards.

The Vibration Test Unit created its own coat of arms, according to the *Bladesman* "in a flight of whimsy." The pineapples and Christmas trees seem to refer to undesirable oscillograph readings.

When America entered the war, the *Bladesman* promised pilots "the finest equipment that aeronautical science can produce. . . . and in such numbers as to enable them to sweep the skies."

Like all war workers, people at the propeller division remembered their goal.

Allied air forces needed engines in acres. The new Ohio plant in Columbus had, according to C-W, "the first conveyor assembly line for aircraft engines."

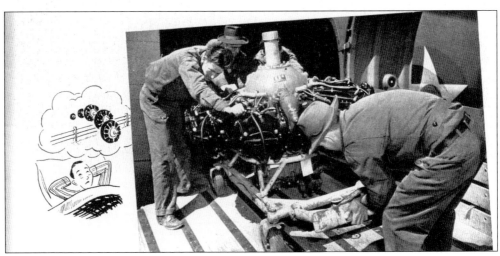

Wright Aeronautical's *Trade Winds* publication imagined a sleepless army maintenance man counting engines instead of sheep.

Curtiss-Wright schools trained mechanics heading overseas to combine precision, speed, and ingenuity.

Pilots got the glamour, but the smart ones knew they would be dead without expert ground crews working daily miracles in horrendous conditions. Wright Cyclone engines such as these, employed on countless Allied aircraft, powered the way to victory.

# *Four*

# KEEP 'EM FLYING!

When World War II exploded, Curtiss-Wright was the only American manufacturer poised for immediate mass production of modern warplanes. The spearhead of C-W's wartime service was 14,000 P-40 Warhawks in various configurations. But the P-40 was flanked by other war-winning airplanes, not to mention mountains of props and acres of engines. In 1942 alone, 140,000 workers kept Curtiss-Wright humming, moving their products into every theater of war, every branch of service, and almost every allied military. On V-J Day, Curtiss-Wright workers celebrated with the rest of the free world, proud that their hands had wrought many of the weapons of victory.

The P-36 ("Mohawk" to the Royal Air Force) was the U.S. Army's first truly successful modern fighter. It was all metal, and had a closed cabin and a low monoplane wing. The fighter was rapidly replaced by the P-40, but the P-36 got into action at Pearl Harbor, the Aleutians, and elsewhere.

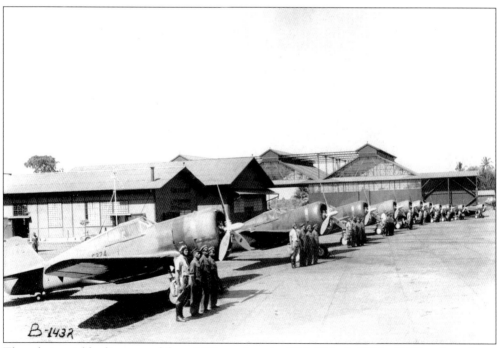

Though it quickly disappeared from U.S. service, the P-36 ("Hawk 75" in C-W parlance) saw combat around the globe, including in China.

A Hawk 75 in the French Armee de l'Air shot down the first German fighter over France. Germany gave captured French Hawks to the Finns for use against the Russians. Curtiss made a thousand Hawks, and some of the export versions used Wright engines.

The O-52 (Curtiss Model 85) Owl was also quickly superseded, as the army recognized that light airplanes such as the Piper Cub could handle observation just as well as heavy two-seaters. Quite a few Owls went to Russia as part of the Lend Lease Act.

Some experiments proved unsuccessful. The pusher-prop Ascender, with its canard elevator in the nose, seemed in some ways like a throwback to the days of Glenn Curtiss and the Wright brothers.

The SOC Seagull float plane was still in use, deployed from cruisers and battleships, when the war started. After completing their missions, generally liaison or reconnaissance, they alighted in the sea to be cranked back aboard. Glenn Curtiss had created the first practical seaplane in 1911, giving birth to naval aviation.

With a liquid-cooled Allison V-12 engine, the P-36 suddenly became an entirely new creation, the Hawk 81 P-40 Warhawk. As quickly as the P-36 had taken over the Army Air Forces, so was it swept away by the P-40.

Critics charged that the P-40 was obsolete the day it rolled off the assembly line, and in some ways they were right. It would have dominated the skies in the Spanish Civil War. But Charles A. Lindbergh found it better than the Bf109 fighter from Messerschmitt, and it had one tremendous advantage—it was ready for mass production.

All around the world, Allied airmen rejoiced when the Warhawks arrived. It meant that they had a chance to fight and live.

Various subtypes were also called Tomahawk or Kittyhawk. British and Commonwealth Desert Rats (the name is scrawled beneath the exhaust pipes) originated the immortal shark's mouth nose art.

Warhawks went into every theater of war, holding the line while superior performers worked their ways from the drawing board to the airstrip.

P-40s were designed to take plenty of punishment, deliver devastating firepower, and bring the pilot home. Two army lieutenants, utterly inexperienced in combat, flew P-40s against both waves of Japanese at Pearl Harbor. Between them they downed seven attackers (out of a total of 29), and landed safely in the end.

Curtiss troubleshooters had to help keep P-40s serviceable in the desert.

They also had to keep them flying in the tropics, in Alaska, in the Aleutians (seen here), and in Russia.

These appear to be Australians at an advanced base, perhaps in New Guinea. The chap with his hands in his pockets must be officer material.

The American Volunteer Group (later known as the "Flying Tigers") adopted both the P-40 and the shark's mouth. Chinese, Americans, and Allies used P-40s throughout the CBI (China-Burma-India) theater.

It was not enough to simply get aircraft to their destinations. Sometimes the very destinations themselves had to be created from scratch. Not only that, but every fighter pilot and fighting warplane took off from an airstrip supported by logistical lines thousands of miles long, carrying everything from bullets and oil to mercurochrome and powdered eggs.

The versatile P-40 was often pressed into service far beyond its intended fighter-bomber role.

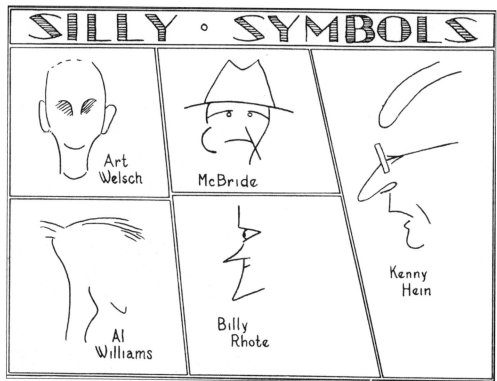

## SILLY · SYMBOLS

Art Welsch

McBride

Kenny Hein

Al Williams

Billy Rhote

Employment ran into tens of thousands at each of numerous Curtiss plants across the country. *Looking Forward,* published in mimeograph by The Aircraft (an independent vertical labor union at Curtiss Buffalo), caricatured some of its own members.

Curtiss workers built over 14,000 P-40s, mostly in Buffalo. Between 20 and 30 countries flew the P-40, or its predecessor, the P-36.

Curtiss production soldiers were fiercely and justifiably proud of their work.

Curtiss hurriedly created the two-seater AT-9 Jeep and rushed it into production just to train pilots of twin-engined bombers and transports. Such aircraft were too scarce during the early years of the war to be wasted on instruction. Once the real thing became available in sufficient numbers, military brass bagged Jeeps for personal transport.

Jeeps on the left, along with SNC-1 advanced naval trainers on the right, "roll off the production lines side by side, day and night, in increasing numbers. . . . in a new airplane plant of the Curtiss-Wright Corporation 'somewhere in the Middle West,'" according to company publicity.

From trainers to operational aircraft, pilots and crewmen across the globe scrambled into Curtiss-Wright cockpits.

The C-76 Curtiss Caravan, a huge all-wood transport plane, arrived too late in the war to make a name for itself.

This laminated wooden spar gives some idea of the Caravan's scale. Curtiss opened a Kentucky plant to handle final assembly.

Vic Arcangelo's Diner at the Buffalo Airport hosted Franklin D. Roosevelt, Wallace Beery, Sonja Heinie, Charles A. Lindbergh, Wiley Post, and Gene Tunney before having to make way for war production.

Mrs. ELEANOR ROOSEVELT congratulates H. LLOYD CHILD, center, while BURDETTE S. WRIGHT looks on. At left:—ROBERT FAUSEL and ED ELLIOTT of the Flight Test section.

Pearl Harbor was still eight months away when Eleanor Roosevelt toured the Buffalo plant with Burdette Wright (far right), taking time to chat with test pilots Robert Fausel (left), Ed Elliott (center), and H. Lloyd Child. "Mrs. Roosevelt showed an unusual knowledge of aircraft manufacturing problems," according to the *Curtiss Flyleaf* internal magazine.

"Mr. President, I feel our plant expansion is getting out of hand"

Frantic expansion provoked C-W to poke fun at itself.

Intricate planning meant that reality was much better organized though just as crowded.

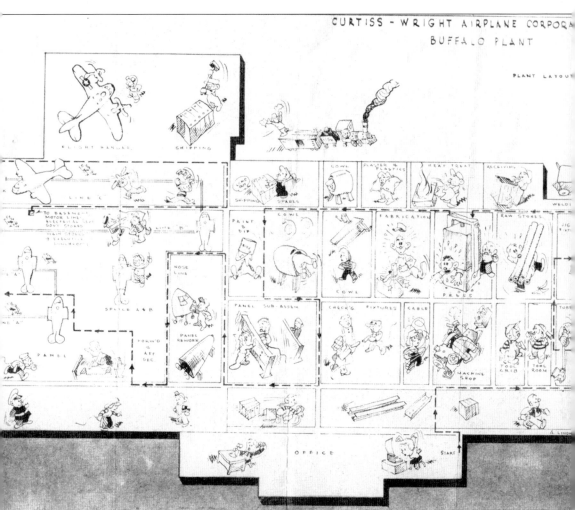

A little humor no doubt helped workers find their way around. A few of the employees had been on the job since the First World War or earlier.

Waste and spoilage delayed victory, but did they misspell "accurate" deliberately?

"Victory boys" as young as 16 (even younger if they were using their big brothers' Social Security cards) worked the Curtiss plants, guided by individual conferences on how to handle factory routine and how to manage big paychecks. Igor Sikorsky told them, "The best planes haven't been thought of—we are just beginning to learn things."

ELECTRICAL ROOM
88-21178-SN    7-31-43

Women in huge numbers worked just about every department.

Office worker Carcella Thompson at the Columbus, Ohio, plant supported the war effort by designing and making her own slacks from remnants.

Viola Browton greeted Pres. Edwin Barclay of Liberia when he visited the press and cutting department in Buffalo. Also visiting that day were president-elect Tubman (who would still be on the job decades later) and Gen. Benjamin O. Davis Sr., "highest-ranking Negro in the U.S. Army." Benjamin Davis Jr. was flying Curtiss P-40s (and later North American P-51 Mustangs) with the Tuskegee Airmen.

Military men training at Camp Curtissair (Army Air Forces Technical Training Center) voted Margaret Gilbert, tool crib clerk at Plant 1, as Miss Warhawk. Men in P-40 squadrons were invited to request eight-by-ten-inch glossies.

# Engineering Cadettes

## of the

## CURTISS-WRIGHT CORPORATION

Curtiss put a thousand women through a year of college training for entry-level positions as engineers. The artist unaccountably pictured a Thunderbolt P-47G in the background, rather than one of Curtiss's own designs. The Buffalo plant built 354 of the Republic fighter-bomber under license.

The non-profit Curtiss Child Care Center charged 50¢ a day to look after children between one and six years of age. The Buffalo-area center accommodated 100 boys and girls under the sponsorship of Mrs. Burdette Wright, whose husband (no relation to Wilbur and Orville, or to engineer T. P. Wright) was vice president in charge of the Airplane Division.

Besides play, supervision, naps, and meals, children got regular nurse examinations—not to mention all the airplane and freight train excitement. Fifty Amherst War Volunteer women assisted salaried staff. A Mrs. Brinkman and a Mrs. Stisser of Red Cross Canteen supervise lunch along with Lera Kidder and Mrs. Herbert O. Fisher. Kidder (a nurse) looks beat.

Numerous women worked for Curtiss as industrial nurses, but women and men alike took first aid training. No matter how up-to-date the new plants were, they still represented a somewhat hazardous environment. Nancy Wilkins and Bessie Keyser were permitted to wear slacks when they demonstrated artificial respiration at the Caldwell, New Jersey plant.

42,000 See How Dad, Mom and the Others help Make War Planes at Curtiss-Ohio

CURTISS-WRIGHT FAMILY DAY

JULY 4, 1943

Despite nostalgia for how everyone pulled together during the war, there is no question that the long struggle strained American families badly. Even so, 42,000 people turned out for this event at the Columbus plant.

Strikes were bad news in wartime. The Labor-Management Committee was designed to minimize problems.

Labor-Management Committees built on experience gained in the First World War and during the New Deal, but did not hold together much past V-J Day.

Barbara Betts kept things swinging as Director of Industrial Music at the propeller plant in New Jersey. She made her selections based on requests from employees and studies by industrial psychologists. Seventy percent of workers preferred fox trots, 10 percent wanted waltzes and polkas, while 8 percent liked swing and 4 percent light opera. Marches, cowboy music, and Latin rhythms tied at 2 percent each.

Bowling leagues were popular in all divisions, while some had musical and stage groups. William deLaar played hockey for the New Jersey propeller division plant.

Attendance, blood donations, bond purchases, and suggestions for improvement all earned points for production soldiers.

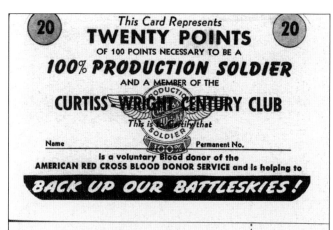

Just keeping track of all the data kept a good-sized workforce busy. The War Production Drive office, which sent out 2,000 forms and letters a month, saved 16 work-hours a month by switching to windowed envelopes.

Public recognition, award pins, and special activities honored those who "made their century" as 100 percent production soldiers. Jim Tranter's subordinates also awarded their boss (right) with a plaque commemorating a lunch in which he stuck the group for $8.

Even office workers put in hard days.

With the gigantic wartime expansion, engineers and managers were stretched to the breaking point.

Company test pilots put their lives on the line day after day after day . . . with suit and tie.

The "Washington office," as it was simply known, included expediters and engineers working closely with the government and the military. They also tracked down out-of-touch service representatives around the globe, hammered out closely rationed airline, railroad, and hotel reservations, and, in one magnificent effort, after a nationwide search, located a mechanical dishwasher for a C-W plant, putting hand washers back on the shop floor.

Contrary to public fantasies about seat-of-the-pants, devil-may-care natural fliers, test pilots survived by being hyper-cautious men who spent a lot of time with facts and figures.

Bill Webster, chief test pilot at Columbus, showed off his "office" to Delmar and Charles Hickey (15 and 16 respectively) on Family Day. Bill's father, C. W. Webster, was a friend and colleague of Glenn Curtiss. C. W. developed Curtiss markets in Latin America, sometimes with the help of spectacular flying by Jimmy Doolittle. Bill died in 2001.

On one occasion, a P-40 test pilot bailed out and the unmanned aircraft crashed into one of the Curtiss plants. This C-46 crash, though spectacular, could have been far worse.

If any landing you walk away from is a good one, this one qualified. Pilot Herb Fisher and C-W fire chief John L. Ward congratulated each other once it was all over.

Curtiss-Wright maintained elaborate fire departments in its many plants.

With thousands of workers and wartime security concerns, the plants also had their own police force.

Many workers went from the factory floor into uniform. Francis D. Metzler of Olean, New York, a radio draftsman at Curtiss Buffalo, became a Marine staff sergeant radio materiel expert on Saipan and Tinian.

The SO3C Seagull (Seamew in Britain) first flew in 1939. Delivery on some 800 U.S. Navy units was completed in January 1944, and the type was so unsatisfactory that it was retired three months later.

The SO3C was supposed to replace the elderly SOC. But many naval vessels actually returned to the old biplane, rather than use the new monoplane with its poor aerodynamics.

The SB2C Helldiver suffered similar problems when first deployed. Angry naval pilots called it "the big-tailed beast" and "Son of a Bitch, Second Class," derived from SB2C. This Helldiver crashed on the carrier *Lexington*.

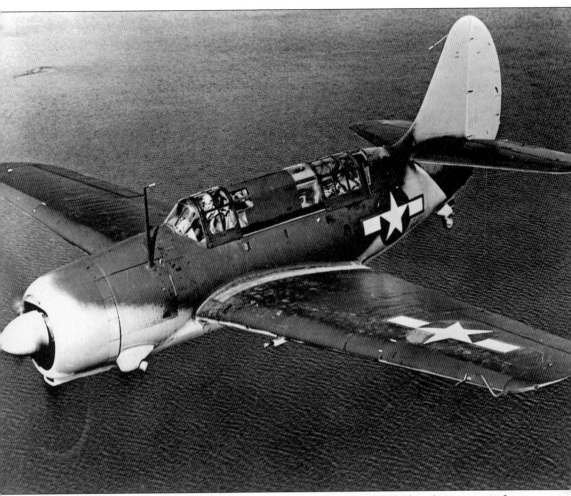

The navy ordered the SB2C, then demanded 800 design changes even before the prototype flew. Teething problems were inevitable.

The two-place dive-bombers, designed specifically for carrier work, first fought at Rabaul. Glenn Curtiss's contract pilot Eugene Ely had worked with the navy to make the first shipboard takeoffs and landings in 1910–1911.

Navy specs demanded too much airplane packed into the relatively small size dictated by carrier deployment. The army bought almost a thousand (as A-25 Shrikes) from the St. Louis plant, then junked their entire dive-bomber program. Shrikes became hot trainers and personal transport for high brass. None were ever used in combat.

Once problems were ironed out, the SB2C quickly became the only dive-bomber in the fleet. Curtiss Columbus built 5,500, while over 1,000 came from licensees in Canada.

The cannon-armed Curtiss Helldiver had Curtiss propellers and, in most cases, Curtiss-Wright engines.

Taking a two-place bomber on and off a bounding carrier deck required superb pilots and a faultless deck crew.

Some of the crew members were even old enough to vote.

Helldivers remained in service until 1949, at the dawn of the jet age.

Far quicker success attended the C-46 (Navy/Marine R5C) Commando cargo/troop transport plane, which already had had extensive development as the civilian CW-20.

Bigger, faster, and higher-flying than the more-numerous C-47 Douglas Dakota, the C-46 could manage startling loads. This was a far cry from Old Number 1, which the Wright brothers had made as the army's first airplane scarcely 30 years before.

Their pressurized cabins and long ranges sent endless streams of Commandoes "over the Hump" of the Himalayas, keeping China in the war against the Japanese.

The army set up an ongoing technical training detachment in Buffalo; this group was brought back from Kunming for six weeks' training on the C-46.

The training detachment (many of whom had already been there) seized on the romance of Himalayan flights.

But even without combat, "the Hump" was one of the world's most dangerous flight zones.

Flying in the CBI (China-Burma-India) Theater had its idiosyncrasies.

On the other hand, what airman would ever forget a flight like this?

Size, speed, range, and pressurization made Commandoes ideal hospital ships.

Marine Maj. Robert B. Meyersburg of Brooklyn, in a Curtiss Commando, was the first pilot to take a full load of wounded from Saipan. In addition to his USMC insignia, Meyersburg wears wings from the Royal Canadian Air Force.

Commandoes also served as glider tow planes.

Army crewmen, many with C-W training and often with help from C-W service representatives, found ways to keep their aircraft flying in the worst of conditions.

"Pat says"

"THIS IS IMPORTANT!"

Read Your Mail . . .

Reply Promptly!!

**SERVICE REPRESENTATIVE'S COLUMN**

by R. PATTINSON
Supervisor of Service
Representatives

R. PATTINSON

Service representatives sent regular bulletins worldwide.

The two-engined Commando had a wider wingspan than the four-engined B-17 "Flying Fortress."

The U.S. military was still using Commandoes in Korea and Vietnam. Dozens, if not hundreds, are still flying worldwide today.

The tough old birds are finishing their careers just as they began—flying vital loads in challenging conditions. In the late 1990s, a single Commando in the Haitian Air Force was the last Curtiss airplane on military service.

During Curtiss-Wright Week, 160,000 people crowded the Buffalo Armory, and rightly so. Between 1936 and 1946, C-W built nearly 30,000 warplanes. In the five war years alone, Curtiss added almost a quarter million engines and 145,000 propellers. But the company that boasted the oldest names in aviation would find its wings badly clipped once the war was won.

# *Five*

# THE SPIRIT
# OF INNOVATION

As victory slashed demand, Curtiss-Wright staggered under its all-but-vacant wartime capital expansion. Shareholders clamored for profits, and the company had fallen behind the design curve, thanks in part to the military's insistence that it concentrate on increasingly outdated models. Postwar work included a jet-powered remote-controlled gunnery target. C-W needed a new mission. Ventures in trailers and in construction equipment died away. Rotary engine and VTOL (vertical takeoff and landing) projects availed little, as did misguided attempts to buy larger companies. After many years of uncertainty, company leaders slowly regained control of Curtiss-Wright's own destiny. Careful expansion and diversification provided a more solid base from which to work. As Glenn Curtiss and the Wright brothers had carried their experience controlling bicycles into controlling airplanes, Curtiss-Wright turned its sights onto control systems and its attitude toward innovation and service.

Six months before the war ended, Curtiss got a navy order for a new carrier-based torpedo bomber using a Wright engine. By the time nine units were delivered in 1946, the need was gone. The XBT2C may be regarded as Curtiss-Wright's last production aircraft, quietly ending a career that had started scarcely 35 years earlier.

The unsuccessful XF15C-1 carrier-based fighter had a DeHavilland-derived jet along with a Pratt and Whitney 18-cylinder conventional engine. The main airframe was built in Buffalo, but the T-tail was added in Columbus. The pilot is believed to be either Lee Miller or Skip Ziegler; Fred Steele was project engineer.

The XP-87 Blackhawk, a night fighter with two Westinghouse jets, showed great promise in 1948. But a military order for 87 additional units was cancelled at the last minute, and North American bought the Aeroplane Division. The Blackhawk prototype (besides being the company's only full jet) was the last manned aircraft from C-W, except for some vertical takeoff and landing experiments in the 1960s.

Nowadays metal treatment is a major part of Curtiss-Wright's work. Shot peening of metal components forestalls fatigue and other deteriorations; it can also be used to induce aerodynamic curvature. In addition to shot peening, C-W's Metal Improvement Company employs heat-treating and laser treating. (Courtesy of Curtiss-Wright Corporation.)

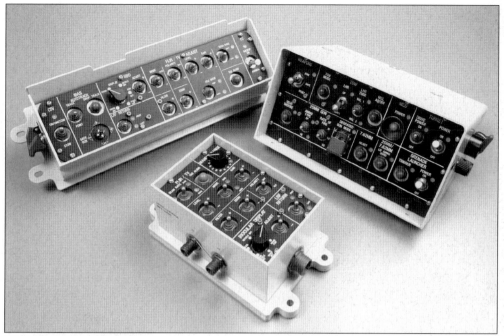

C-W Embedded Computing makes rugged mission-critical control systems that serve such weapons as the Bradley Fighting Vehicle and the Abrams Main Battle Tank. (Courtesy of Curtiss-Wright Corporation.)

The Mission Management Computer is the "brains" for Northrop Grumman Ryan's Global Hawk Unmanned Aerial Vehicle, which provides high-resolution intelligence and surveillance for the U.S. Air Force. (Courtesy of Curtiss-Wright Corporation.)

Curtiss-Wright was the primary provider of main propulsion systems, shipboard electrical power generation, and critical shipboard pumping and valve equipment for the aircraft carrier *Ronald Reagan*. Celebrating together on December 31, 2004, from left to right, are Michael J. Denton (vice president, corporate secretary, general counsel), Glenn E. Tynan (vice president-finance, treasurer, CFO), David J. Linton (president Curtiss-Wright Flow Control), Martin R. Benante (chairman and CEO), George J. Yohrling (president Curtiss-Wright Motion Control), and Edward Bloom (president Curtiss-Wright Metal Treatment). Benante assumed office in 2000. (Courtesy of Curtiss-Wright Corporation.)

Curtiss-Wright still takes to the skies with flight controls, utility actuators, and integrated systems serving airplanes and helicopters, both commercial and military. The highly successful Curtiss-Wright Power Hinge rotary actuator, originally created for the B-70 Valkyre, controls active leading edge flaps on the Lockheed Martin/Boeing F-22 Next Generation Air Superiority Fighter. (Courtesy of Curtiss-Wright Corporation.)

DeltaValve, a business unit of Curtiss-Wright Flow Control, makes coker valves. Curtiss-Wright is an industry leader in leakless valves for nuclear and non-nuclear applications. (Courtesy of Curtiss-Wright Corporation.)

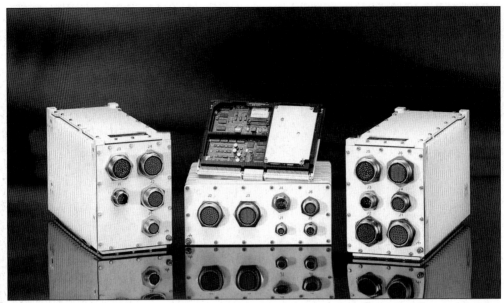

C-W Embedded Computing makes turret control electronics for the 105 millimeter Stryker Mobile Gun System. (Courtesy of Curtiss-Wright Corporation.)

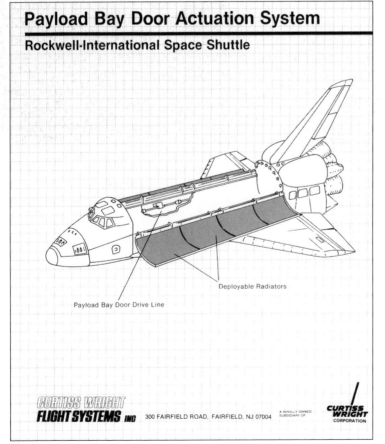

## Payload Bay Door Actuation System

### Rockwell-International Space Shuttle

Deployable Radiators

Payload Bay Door Drive Line

CURTISS WRIGHT
**FLIGHT SYSTEMS INC** 300 FAIRFIELD ROAD, FAIRFIELD, NJ 07004  A WHOLLY OWNED SUBSIDIARY OF

**CURTISS WRIGHT** CORPORATION

When the space shuttle *Columbia* deployed satellites into orbit, Curtiss-Wright actuators opened those great doors to the vastness of space. It is unlikely that either Glenn Curtiss or the Wright brothers ever dreamed of such a marvel—and it is unlikely that any of us dream what heights Curtiss-Wright will reach in the second century of flight. (Courtesy of Curtiss-Wright Corporation.)

As flight's first century drew to a close, *Aviation Week and Space Technology* named 100 stars of aerospace. Glenn Curtiss was honored in fifth place, right behind Leonardo da Vinci, Robert Goddard, Werner von Braun, and, of course, the Wright brothers. Chairman and CEO Martin Benante represented C-W in accepting Glenn Curtiss's award at ceremonies in Paris. The author had the honor of speaking immediately afterward on behalf of Mrs. Glenn Curtiss Jr. (Courtesy of Curtiss-Wright Corporation.)

As the company rounded the dawn of the 21st century, the centennial of flight, and its own 75th birthday, Curtiss-Wright rekindled its success by reprising the innovative entrepreneurial enthusiasm of the oldest names in aviation. In hostile skies, on disputed ground, in ocean depths, and even in the immensity of space, Curtiss and Wright are still making their marks. (Courtesy of Curtiss-Wright Corporation.)